Do Tigers Ha Live

Written by

Sally Grindley

Illustrated by

Jago

OXFORD
UNIVERSITY PRESS

OXFORD
UNIVERSITY PRESS

Great Clarendon Street, Oxford, OX2 6DP, United Kingdom

Oxford University Press is a department of the University of Oxford.
It furthers the University's objective of excellence in research, scholarship,
and education by publishing worldwide. Oxford is a registered trade mark
of Oxford University Press in the UK and in certain other countries

Text © Sally Grindley 2015
Illustrations © Oxford University Press 2015

British Library Cataloguing in Publication Data
Data available

ISBN: 978-0-19-835678-3

10 9 8 7 6 5 4 3 2

Paper used in the production of this book is a natural, recyclable product
made from wood grown in sustainable forests. The manufacturing process
conforms to the environmental regulations of the country of origin.

Printed in China by Leo Paper Products Ltd

Acknowledgements

Series Advisor: Nikki Gamble
Illustrated by Jago
Designed by Oxford University Press in collaboration with Ana Cosma

Chapter 1

I still remember my seventh birthday, when my grandpa gave me a tiger.

He was a soft tiger, a whiskery tiger, a tiger with big black eyes that shone in the light.

He was my best present and I kept him with me all day long. He was with me when I unwrapped my other presents and blew out my candles, and when everyone sang 'Happy Birthday' to me.

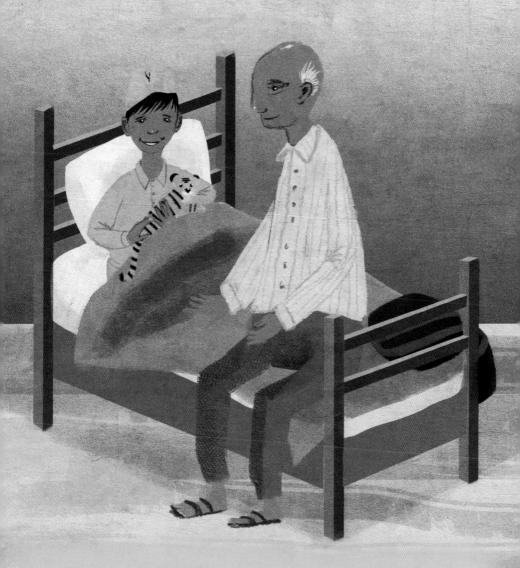

At bedtime, Grandpa laid the tiger by my side. "Do tigers have nine lives, Grandpa?" I asked him.

"Well, tigers belong to the cat family so perhaps they do," Grandpa replied.

I stroked my tiger while Grandpa told me
all about real tigers. "They live in forests and
jungles, and they love to swim," he said.
"Each tiger's stripes are unique, just like our
fingerprints."

And then he added sadly, "There are very
few tigers left in the wild."

Grandpa kissed me goodnight, then turned off the light. My tiger seemed to move closer as I shut my eyes. I held one of his paws as I drifted into my dreams.

Chapter 2

I must have been asleep for a while, when suddenly I felt warm breath on my cheek. A huge paw gently nudged me awake. My tiger stood by the side of my bed, gazing at my face. He was a strong tiger, a bold tiger, a tiger with golden eyes that gleamed like stars.

My tiger walked towards the open window
and I knew at once that he wanted to leave.
"Can I come with you?" I asked. I was
worried that I would never see him again.

He waited, pacing up and
down as I pulled on my
dressing gown and slippers.

I clambered onto my tiger's enormous back. Seconds later, he leaped through the window, then padded across the road and raced off into the night.

He ran so fast that I had to hold on tight. I wrapped my arms firmly around his neck and felt the power of his mighty muscles. His chest rose and fell as he breathed.

On and on he ran, through towns and cities ...

... through woodlands and fields,

over hills and mountains ...

... across rivers and by the sea.

He ran on and on, until the air became
warmer and the night sky melted into daylight.

Roads turned into dusty tracks, and trees
became thick jungle.

Chapter 3

At last, my tiger slowed to a walk. I
climbed down from his back and walked
beside him.

"Where are we?" I asked but he was too
busy sniffing the air to pay attention to me.
I stroked his nose and gazed around.

The sights and smells of the jungle filled my head. Above us, we could hear creatures in the treetops chattering and screeching. I spotted a monkey peering through the branches. It screamed and rushed away as soon as it saw us.

My tiger led me deeper into the jungle. Soon
we came to a small waterhole, where groups
of gazelles were drinking. They leaped in panic
when they saw my tiger and disappeared into
the bushes. My tiger didn't chase them and I
was glad.

My tiger walked into the water and began to swim. He swam so easily and was so happy that I knew he had come home to the country of his birth. I was proud to have been invited there, and I called out to my tiger,

"Thank you for bringing me with you!"

I watched him in wonder. At last he climbed out of the water and shook himself dry. We continued slowly on our way and my tiger looked carefully at everything we passed.

As the afternoon grew hotter, my tiger lay
down under the shade of a tree and slept.
I rested my head on his back but I was much
too excited to sleep. I had never been anywhere
like this! I wanted to remember every last smell
and sight and sound.

I set off to explore.

I saw ants carrying leaves much larger than
themselves, and butterflies as big as my hand.
I smiled as a large brown bird stepped through
a tangle of twigs, saw me and dashed
away again.

I watched in amazement as a stick insect walked along a narrow branch and then disappeared from sight, as if by magic.

I hadn't gone far when I heard a strange
sound above the calls and cries of the jungle.
I listened hard, trying to work out what could
be making the sound. It didn't seem to
belong there.

I peered through the trees, trying to find out what was making the noise. It grew louder as I moved forward. There were no butterflies flitting around here, no animals sniffing for food. Everything was still, so still. All I could hear was that terrible noise. Suddenly I saw clear ground up ahead.

Chapter 4

I walked out into the open. In front of me was a huge area of bare and devastated ground. It looked as if a tornado had hit it and destroyed everything in its path.

In the distance, massive machines
ploughed backwards and forwards,
knocking down everything that stood in
their way. More trees were being ripped
from their roots by the machines, stripped
of their branches and laid in neat piles.

"Stop!" I cried angrily. I started to run
towards the machines. My tiger woke up
and raced to my side. He stared out over the
devastated landscape and let out a deep roar
of pain. The land he'd loved as a cub had been
completely destroyed.

I threw my arms around his neck and tried to comfort him, almost crying myself. But he shook himself free. He began to walk over the shattered ground, sniffing anxiously as he went.

He moved more quickly, lurching from side to side and growling loudly. I realized he was searching for signs of his family.

And then he stopped. He lifted his
magnificent head and roared a terrible roar.

In that moment,
the rest of the world
seemed to fall silent.

I wanted to comfort my tiger but there was nothing I could say or do. He turned, took one last look at what remained of his home, then lowered his head and began to walk away.

As he did, there was a shudder of leaves and a crackle of twigs. All of a sudden, another tiger burst through the bushes.

I couldn't believe my eyes!

Chapter 5

It was a female tiger. She ran to my tiger and greeted him. He stared at her, amazed, and swished his tail. Then he nuzzled her cheek and rolled onto his back, as if asking her to play.

The two tigers played like young cubs.

They leaped and frolicked
and tumbled and chased.

I was tempted to join in but this was their
moment. I was happy to stand and watch instead.

The tigers scampered backwards and forwards across the shattered land. Then they suddenly turned and disappeared through the trees. I ran after them but they were nowhere to be found.

My heart sank. I feared that I would never see
my tiger again.

I sat and waited. Now the jungle sounds
made me feel frightened and very alone.

At last, from deep within the forest, I heard my tiger roar. I jumped to my feet and wished he would come back to me.

But I wasn't the only one to hear him.

I caught the sound of voices nearby and saw a group of men striding into the forest. I knew at once that the tigers were in great danger.

Chapter 6

"Run!" I screamed. I couldn't let the men harm my tiger.

Shots rang out. I screamed again. "Run!"

Suddenly, my tiger crashed through the bushes, knocking me off my feet. I climbed on his back and held on tight as he charged away through the trees.

More shots rang out. As my tiger ran, I looked around for his friend. "Please let her be safe," I whispered. I spotted a flash of stripes. There she was!

She was fast – so fast! I held my breath and then cried with relief when I saw she had escaped.

On and on my tiger ran. The dense jungle gave way to dusty tracks as the sun went down and twilight moved in.

We ran by seas and rivers, and climbed over mountains and hills.

We travelled across fields and woodlands, and passed through cities and towns.

On and on my tiger ran, while the air became
cooler and darkness fell. As we fled through the
night, I rested my head on my tiger's back and
slept. It was a sleep of dreams – tiger dreams.

When I opened my eyes, Grandpa was sitting beside me. Sunlight was streaming through my bedroom window.

"Wakey, wakey, sleepyhead," he said.

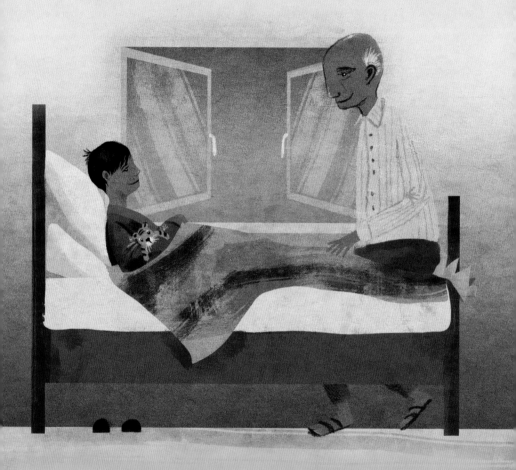

For a moment, I didn't know where I was.
I shivered, remembering the men and the shots and the machines.

I reached for my tiger and was relieved to find that he was lying next to me. I picked him up and held him to my face. I could almost feel him nuzzle my cheek.

"I think he lost one of his lives in the night," I told Grandpa, stroking the fur around my tiger's ears. "He had a lucky escape."

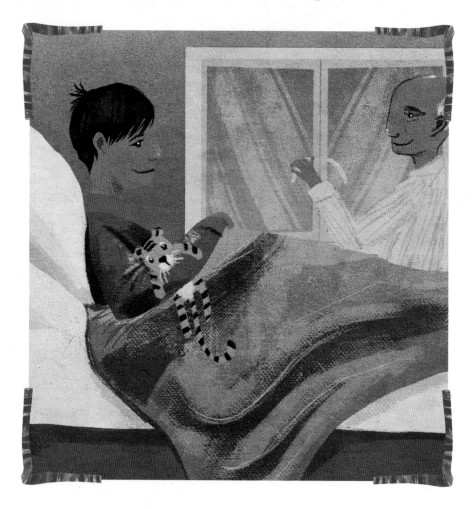

Grandpa closed the window. "We'll have to make sure he doesn't lose any more," he said, with a knowing smile.